Speech Bubbles 2 User Guide

This book is the supporting guide for *Speech Bubbles 2*, an exciting series created for speech language pathologists, parents and caregivers, teachers and other professionals working with children with disordered speech sound development. The guide contains detailed notes to support the effective use of all the picture books in the series, targeting the following sounds: /v/, /z/, /sh/, /ch/, /h/, /y/, /j/, /r/, /l/, /w/, /r/ blends and /l/ blends.

Speech Bubbles 2 is the second set in a series of picture books designed to be used by those working with children who have delayed or disordered speech sound development, children receiving speech therapy or those wanting to provide sound awareness activities for children. The set includes 12 beautifully illustrated storybooks, each targeting a different speech sound in different positions within words, and a user guide with notes on each individual story. Designed to be read aloud to the child in a therapy, classroom or home setting, the stories create a fun and engaging activity that can be returned to again and again.

The full set includes:

- Twelve bright and engaging stories targeting the following early developing sounds and sounds frequently targeted in speech therapy: /v/, /z/, /sh/, /ch/, /h/, /y/, /j/, /r/, /l/, /w/, /r/ blends and /l/ blends.

- A user guide supporting the use of the stories, with individual notes on each.

Perfect not just for therapy but also for encouraging early sound awareness and development, this is an engaging and invaluable resource for speech language therapists and pathologists, parents and caregivers and teachers working with children aged 2–8 years.

Melissa Palmer is a Speech Language Therapist. She worked for the Ministry of Education, Special Education in New Zealand from 2008 to 2013, with children aged primarily between 2 and 8 years of age. She also completed a diploma in children's writing in 2009, studying under author Janice Marriott, through the New Zealand Business Institute. Melissa has a passion for articulation and phonology, as well as writing and art, and has combined these two loves to create *Speech Bubbles*.

What's in the pack?

User Guide

Vinnie the Dove

Rick's Carrot

Harry the Hopper

Have You Ever Met a Yeti?

Zack the Buzzy Bee

Asher the Thresher Shark

Catch That Chicken!

Will the Wolf

Magic Licking Lollipops

Jasper the Badger

Platypus and Fly

The Dragon Drawing War

Speech Bubbles 2 User Guide

Supporting Speech Sound Development in Children

Melissa Palmer

Routledge
Taylor & Francis Group

LONDON AND NEW YORK

First published 2021
by Routledge
2 Park Square, Milton Park, Abingdon, Oxon OX14 4RN

and by Routledge
52 Vanderbilt Avenue, New York, NY 10017

Routledge is an imprint of the Taylor & Francis Group, an informa business

British Library Cataloguing-in-Publication Data
A catalogue record for this book is available from the British Library

Library of Congress Cataloging-in-Publication Data
Names: Palmer, Melissa (Speech language therapist), author.
Title: Speech bubbles 2 user guide : supporting speech sound development in children / Melissa Palmer. Other titles: Speech bubbles two user guide
Description: Abingdon, Oxon ; New York, N.Y. : Routledge, 2021.
Identifiers: LCCN 2020047769 (print) | LCCN 2020047770 (ebook) |
ISBN 9780367648473 (paperback) | ISBN 9781003126539 (ebook)
Subjects: LCSH: Speech therapy for children—Handbooks, manuals, etc. |
Articulation disorders in children—Handbooks, manuals, etc.
Classification: LCC LB3454 .P333 2019 (print) |
LCC LB3454 (ebook) | DDC 371.91/42–dc23
LC record available at https://lccn.loc.gov/2020047769
LC ebook record available at https://lccn.loc.gov/2020047770

ISBN: 978-1-138-59784-6 (set)
ISBN: 978-0-367-64847-3 (pbk)
ISBN: 978-1-003-12653-9 (ebk)

Typeset in Calibri
by Newgen Publishing UK

Printed in the UK by Severn, Gloucester on responsibly sourced paper

For William and Oliver

Contents

Contents

Introduction

This is the second pack of picture books in the *Speech Bubbles* series designed to target specific sounds in children's speech sound development.

Just like the first pack, this pack is designed to be used with children aged predominantly between 2 and 8 years old. This age range is when children typically develop a wide range of speech sounds used in their speech.

In this pack, you will find 12 picture books and this user guide. The sounds targeted are: /v/, /z/, /sh/, /ch/, /h/, /y/, /j/, /r/, /l/, /w/, /r/ blends and /l/ blends. This range includes early developing sounds, as well as sounds that are frequently targeted in speech therapy during the early years. Please refer to the first *Speech Bubbles* pack for eleven additional picture books targeting different speech sounds. The assorted titles are now also available to be purchased individually.

These books can be used by speech language therapists/pathologists, teachers and parents/caregivers. The stories are designed to be read aloud to the child by an adult. This enables the adult to draw attention to the target sound, and to provide a correct model for the child to hear multiple times and in different positions within a word. This includes the sound by itself (in isolation), the beginning of words (in initial position), in middle position (medial position) and at the end of words (final position). It also provides a model of what these words then sound like within sentences. Children love to read stories again and again, and this process of repetition gives the child lots of exposure to the target sound.

Each story targets a specific speech sound. The target sound has been underlined and made bold to bring attention to it within each story, so the reader is guided to where to place emphasis while reading. Please note that while letters are underlined in the stories, it is not the letters that are the target, it is the sound they make. Blends (which are two consonant sounds together without a vowel in between) with the target sound in them are not underlined, as these are much more difficult to pronounce. The exceptions to this are *The Dragon Drawing War* and *Platypus and Fly*, which target /r/ blends and /l/ blends specifically. Please refer to the notes on each individual story for more information.

These books are not designed to replace receiving speech language therapy when necessary; they were developed to be used alongside speech therapy, as a tool. They can also be used as a fun and engaging activity to promote speech sound development for children within the home as well as at schools, kindergartens and centres.

If you have concerns about your child's speech sound development, please refer to a Speech Language Therapist/Pathologist for an assessment.

USeS

For speech language therapists/ pathologists

These picture books are designed to be used as an activity for during the therapy session, or to be sent home as 'homework' with families of a child receiving therapy.

They are designed to be used as an auditory bombardment type activity, especially for those children who are reluctant to participate in therapy. This way, it is a non-confrontational activity where the child first listens, but is not expected to use the target sound themselves or repeat words etc. If the child is comfortable repeating sounds and words, then the books could also be used for this as well.

The chosen sound is targeted in initial, medial and final position and also in isolation so it can be used as an activity no matter what stage of therapy the child is at currently.

The target sound is underlined and made in bold to draw attention to it, but is a guideline only. These words could potentially be used as target words, which you could get the child to repeat after you, or once they are more familiar with the story, you could pause while reading and they say the word themselves. In this way, you can use the story throughout the stages of therapy – e.g. if targeting the sound in isolation, encourage the child to make the target sound at the appropriate moment of the story. If you are targeting a sound in initial position, focus on those words in the story and ask the child to say the word. This can work when targeting two-word phrases and then longer sentences.

The sounds underlined are those that are in more simple words e.g. no blends or clusters. However, in the majority of the books, these more difficult words are still included and could also be targeted should you choose. Both single syllable and two to three syllable words have also been included in the underlining, so there is also the possibility of further simplifying your targets if required.

For parents/caregivers and teachers

This series of picture books is designed predominantly as a listening activity for the children. The purpose is for the adult to read the story with the chosen target sound to the child, giving the child many different and correct examples of how to use the sound, and the sound within words and sentences. If being used as a listening activity, the child would not be expected to participate in the story e.g. repeating words or sounds after you, but rather would listen to how you use the sound within the words and story. The repetition of the target sound within words increases the frequency to which the child hears the sound. The more the child hears it, the more likely they will hear the difference between what they are currently using and the correct pronunciation of the sound/word. This makes this picture book series also very useful for those children who are shy, and those who may be aware that people find them hard to understand and are reluctant to participate in a sound awareness activity themselves.

If the child is willing to participate, you may like to ask them to repeat a word or sound after you, or if the child is familiar with the story, pause to see if they will fill in the gap. If the child uses the sound correctly, be sure to praise them with positive reinforcement e.g. "Good talking, that was a great /sh/ sound." If they don't use it correctly, do not say anything negative e.g. "That was wrong, you say it like this." Negative feedback may cause the child to not participate at all, and the aim of the picture books is to create a fun, positive and relaxed learning environment. Focus on the positive, and ignore the negative.

As you look through the books, you will notice that letters have been underlined and made in bold throughout the story. It's important to remember that this is to draw your attention to the <u>sound</u> these letters make, not the actual letters themselves. For example, in the story that targets the /y/ sound, you will see that the letters 'i' and 'a' have been underlined in the word 'giant'. This is because in these circumstances, those letters make a /y/ sound within that word. You may notice as you go through the stories, that there will be occasions that letters are not underlined where you may initially think they should be. This may be because the letters are not pronounced as the target sound e.g. in the story targeting the /h/ sound, the letter 'h' would not be underlined at the end of the word 'high' as it is not pronounced as a /h/ sound. It is, however, underlined at the beginning of that particular word.

Another thing to note is that during the story, if the target sound occurs in a blend – which is where two consonant sounds are made together within a word without a vowel in between e.g. /sp/ in 'spoon' – the sound has not been underlined. This is because blends are much harder to use than a single consonant sound by itself. For this reason, there are specific stories targeting common blends in English separately. Within this pack, there are two stories targeting common blends – *The Dragon Drawing War* targeting /r/ blends, and *Platypus and Fly* targeting /l/ blends. Please see the individual pages with notes for each separate book for more details.

If using these picture books without the guidance of a Speech Language Therapist/Pathologist (SLT/P), it is recommended that you use the books as a listening and sound awareness activity. You may like to ask the child to repeat a sound or word after you, but do not place any pressure on the child to do so. If the child has difficulty producing certain speech sounds, and doesn't appear to be improving, it would be advisable to get an assessment from a SLT/P and use the stories in a way that fits into the child's therapy plan.

Notes for individual picture books

Vinnie the Dove - Targeting the /v/ Sound

- While reading the story to the child, you could occasionally point out the /v/ sound e.g. "Vinnie started to shiver" ... "Oh, Vinnie starts with a /v/ sound."

- You could talk about how you make the sound e.g. "I touch my top teeth to my bottom lip and blow out, turning my voice on ... /v/."

- You could get the child to watch <u>you</u> make the /v/ sound and use a mirror so they can see if they are doing the same as you.

- If the child repeats the word or sound after you correctly, be sure to praise them e.g. "Well done, that was a great /v/ sound." Be sure to focus on the positive rather than the negative – don't point out their mistakes.

Underlined /v/ sound by position in words

Initial (beginning)	Medial (middle)	Final (end)
Vinnie	Diving	Dove (animal)
Very	River	Dove (action)
Vicious	Shiver	Cave
Vest	Beaver	Dave
	Shivering	Glove
	Oven	
	Covered	
	Clever	

Not underlined

Word (reason underlined)	Reason
Lo**ved** Li**ved**	Two consonants together (or a blend)

Rick's Carrot - Targeting the /r/ Sound

- While reading the story to the child, you could occasionally point out the /r/ sound e.g. "Rick the rabbit was really hungry" … "oh, rabbit starts with a /r/ sound."

- You could talk about how <u>you</u> make the sound e.g. "I touch the middle of my tongue to the sides of my teeth and curl the tip a bit … /r/."

- You could get the child to watch <u>you</u> make the /r/ sound, and use a mirror so they can see if they are doing the same as you.

- If the child repeats the word or sound after you correctly, be sure to praise them e.g. "Well done, that was a great /r/ sound." Be sure to focus on the positive rather than the negative – don't point out their mistakes.

- You will notice that /r/ in the final position of words has been included. It depends on where you are from and what accent you have as to whether or not this needs to be targeted. In New Zealand, the /r/ sound is not pronounced at the end of words – rather it is left off all together. Therefore, it does not need to focused on at all there. In America, /r/ is produced in the final position of words, and so it may be an appropriate target there.

Underlined /r/ sound by position in words

Initial (beginning)	Medial (middle)	Final (end)
Rick	Orange	Under
Rabbit	Carrot	Over
Really	Very	Robber
Ripe	Giraffe	There
Rock	Terry	Your
Robbed	Parrot	Alligator
Robber	Were	River
Roared	Cherries	After
Randy	Sorry	Her
Reaching		For
Resting		Together
Roof		Share
Rebecca		
Relaxing		
River		
Rumble		
Right		
Ran		
Red		
Ralph		
Rat		
Realise		
Rest		

Not underlined

Word (reason underlined)	Reason
Hun**gr**y	Two consonants together without a vowel in between (or a blend)
Forwa**rd**	
Tu**rned**	
An**gr**y	
Tree	
Try	
Sca**red**	
Sha**rp**	
Al**r**eady	

Harry the Hopper - Targeting the /h/ Sound

- While reading the story to the child, you could occasionally point out the /h/ sound e.g. "Harry the hopper loved to hop" ... "oh, hopper starts with a /h/ sound."

- You could talk about how <u>you</u> make the sound e.g. "I blow out my breath really quietly like this ... /h/."

- You could get the child to watch you make the /h/ sound, and use a mirror so they can see if they are doing the same as you.

- If the child repeats the word or sound after you correctly, be sure to praise them e.g. "Well done, that was a great /h/ sound." Be sure to focus on the positive rather than the negative – don't point out their mistakes.

- /h/ is only targeted in the beginning of words in this story – this is usually where it occurs rather than the other positions. It is also targeted as the sound by itself.

Underlined /h/ sound in words

Initial (beginning)	Medial (middle)	Final (end)
Harry		
Hopper		
Hop		
He		
Hopped		
High		
Happy		
Hopefully		
Hopping		
Have		
Hello		
Who		
Hannah		
Huff		
Help		
Her		
House		
Held		
Hands		

Not underlined

Word (reason underlined)	Reason
Gras**sh**opper	Two consonants together without a vowel in between
T**h**e Thou**gh**t T**h**ey Toge**th**er Hi**gh** S**h**ow Hanna**h** T**h**ere Suc**h** **Th**ing S**h**e Splas**h** T**h**ank Bot**h**	Not produced as a /h/ sound

Have You Ever Met a Yeti? - Targeting the /y/ Sound

- While reading the story to the child, you could occasionally point out the /y/ sound e.g. "Have you ever seen a yeti" ... "oh, yeti starts with a /y/ sound."

- You could talk about how <u>you</u> make the sound e.g. "I lift my tongue up at the back and down at the front ... /y/."

- You could get the child to watch you make the /y/ sound, and use a mirror so they can see if they are doing the same as you.

- If the child repeats the word or sound after you correctly, be sure to praise them e.g. "Well done, that was a great /y/ sound." Be sure to focus on the positive rather than the negative – don't point out their mistakes.

- /y/ is targeted at the beginning and middle of words in this book as it doesn't normally occur at the ends of words. Please note that the letter 'y' may be at the end of a word, but it is not pronounced as a /y/ sound. The sound by itself is also in the story.

Underlined /y/ sound within words

Initial (beginning)	Medial (middle)	Final (end)
You	Giant	
Yeti	Carrying	
Yellow	Onions	
Young	Brian	
Yams	Lying	
Yolk	Fuzziest	
Yummy	Scariest	
Yell	Funniest	
Yurt		
Yawn		
Yarny		
Yak		
Yarny's		
Yeti's		
Year		
Unicorn		

Not underlined

Word (reason underlined)	Reason
Tumm**y**	Not produced as a /y/ sound
Particularl**y**	
Yumm**y**	
E**y**es	
Yarn**y**	
Ma**y**be	

Zack the Buzzy Bee - Targeting the /z/ Sound

- While reading the story to the child, you could occasionally point out the /z/ sound e.g. "Just then he saw a lizard, who was just about to sneeze" … "oh, lizard has a /z/ sound in it."

- You could talk about how <u>you</u> make the sound e.g. "I touch my tongue up to the top of my mouth behind your teeth. Blow out your breath, and turn your voice on … /z/."

- You could get the child to watch you make the /z/ sound, making sure the tongue is down at the front, and use a mirror so they can see if they are doing the same as you.

- If the child repeats the word or sound after you correctly, be sure to praise them e.g. "Well done, that was a great /z/ sound." Be sure to focus on the positive rather than the negative – don't point out their mistakes.

- You will notice that sometimes an /s/ on the ends of words is produced more as a /z/ sound. These words have been included as targets as shown below.

Underlined /z/ sound within words

Initial (beginning)	Medial (middle)	Final (end)
Zen	Lazily	Breeze
Zoomed	Fuzzy	His
Zebra	Buzzy	Was
Zip	Puzzling	Please
Zoom	Lizard	Bees
Zack	Guzzling	Cheese
Zapped	Daisy	Is
Zig zag	Lazy	Size
Zooming	Squeezing	Goodbyes
Zack's	Drizzled	Sneeze
Zucchinis		Excuse
Zig zagging		Daze
		Zucchinis
		Bodies
		Liz

Asher the Thresher Shark - Targeting the /sh/ Sound

- While reading the story to the child, you could occasionally point out the /sh/ sound e.g. "Asher the thresher shark" … "oh, shark starts with a /sh/ sound."

- You could talk about how <u>you</u> make the sound e.g. "I make my lips like kissing lips then blow out, using a quiet sound … /sh/." You could hold your finger up in front of your mouth and make the 'quiet sound' – a shushing sound.

- You could get the child to watch you make the /sh/ sound, and use a mirror so they can see if they are doing the same as you.

- If the child repeats the word or sound after you correctly, be sure to praise them e.g. "Well done, that was a great /sh/ sound." Be sure to focus on the positive rather than the negative – don't point out their mistakes.

- You will notice that 'c' and 't' are also underlined in a couple of words. That's because in those words, they are pronounced as a /sh/ sound.

Underlined /sh/ sound within words

Initial (beginning)	Medial (middle)	Final (end)
Shark	Asher	Fish
Sharks	Thresher	Dish
Share	Ocean	Push
Shy	Commotion	Splash
Shot	Dashing	Trash
Sharp	Splashing	Dash
Shimmering	Pushing	Smash
Shooting	Push	Rubbish
Shining		
Shoe		
Shirt		
Shyness		
Shouting		
Shyly		

Not underlined

Word (reason underlined)	Reason
Pu**shed** Gu**shed**	Two consonant sounds together without a vowel in between (or in blend)

Catch That Chicken! - Targeting the /ch/ Sound

- While reading the story to the child, you could occasionally point out the /ch/ sound e.g. "Charlie the ostrich" … "oh, ostrich ends with a /ch/ sound."

- You could talk about how <u>you</u> make the sound e.g. "I touch the tip of my tongue to the roof of my mouth, behind my teeth, and then blow out like a /sh/ sound … /ch/."

- You could get the child to watch you make the /ch/ sound, and use a mirror so they can see if they are doing the same as you.

- If the child repeats the word or sound after you correctly, be sure to praise them e.g. "Well done, that was a great /ch/ sound." Be sure to focus on the positive rather than the negative – don't point out their mistakes.

Underlined /ch/ sound within words

Initial (beginning)	Medial (middle)	Final (end)
Charlie	Archie	Ostrich
Cherished	Nacho	Patch
Chose	Nachos	Which
Cherries	Pitcher	Spinach
Chicken		Catch
Check		Beach
Cherry		Peach
Cheeping		
Charged		
Charlie's		
Chased		
Chips		
Cheese		
Chocolate		
Chatter		
Chilly		
Chattering		
Chugged		
Children		

Not underlined

Word (reason underlined)	Reason/explanation
Mun**ched** Sea**rch**ing Cru**nch**y Lur**ched** Pin**ched** Rea**ched** Clut**ched** Lu**nch** Scrat**ched**	Two consonant sounds together without a vowel in between (blend)
Pi**nched**	More than two consonant sounds together without a vowel in between (a cluster)

will the Wolf - Targeting the /w/ Sound

- While reading the story to the child, you could occasionally point out the /w/ sound e.g. "Will the wolf loved to watch the world going on around him" … "oh, wolf starts with a /w/ sound."

- You could talk about how <u>you</u> make the sound e.g. "I purse my lips like kissing lips and then relax them like this. I also turn my voice on … /w/."

- You could get the child to watch you make the /w/ sound, and use a mirror so they can see if they are doing the same as you.

- If the child repeats the word or sound after you correctly, be sure to praise them e.g. "Well done, that was a great /w/ sound." Be sure to focus on the positive rather than the negative – don't point out their mistakes.

- The /w/ sound is targeted in the beginning and middle of words in the story. Although the letter 'w' is often at the end of words, it is generally not pronounced as a /w/ sound. It is therefore not targeted in the story. The sound by itself is also included in the story.

Underlined /w/ sound within words

Initial (beginning)	Medial (middle)	Final (end)
Will	Going	
Wolf	Away	
Watch	Blowing	
World	Awake	
When	Powerful	
Wet		
Watched		
Was		
Windy		
Went		
Wood		
Water		
Wheel		
Wagon		
Weeds		
Worm		
Wiggle		
Wind		
Washing		
Whales		
Waves		
While		

Initial (beginning)	Medial (middle)	Final (end)
With		
Wonder		
What		
One		
Wonderful		
Wolves		
White		
Willa		
Watching		

Not underlined

Word (reason underlined)	Reason/explanation
Ho**wled**	Two consonant sounds together without a vowel in between (blend)
Sa**w** Follo**w**	'w' at the end of the word – not produced as a /w/ sound

Magic Licking Lollipops - Targeting the /l/ Sound

- While reading the story to the child, you could occasionally point out the /l/ sound e.g. "Lynn loved to lick lollipops" … "oh, loved starts with a /l/ sound."

- You could talk about how <u>you</u> make the sound e.g. "I touch the tip of my tongue to the roof of my mouth and roll it. I also turn my voice on … /l/."

- You could get the child to watch you make the /l/ sound, and use a mirror so they can see if they are doing the same as you.

- If the child repeats the word or sound after you correctly, be sure to praise them e.g. "Well done, that was a great /l/ sound." Be sure to focus on the positive rather than the negative – don't point out their mistakes.

Underlined /l/ sound within words

Initial (beginning)	Medial (middle)	Final (end)
Lynn	Lollipops	Roll
Loved	Lily	Little
Lick	Little	Full
Lollipops	Lolly	All
Liked	Alan's	Will
Looked	Lollies	You'll
Lily	Yellow	Normal
Little	Coloured	
Lolly	Alan	
Long	Lollipop	
Lollies	Colours	
Let's	Slowly	
Look	Colour	
Lots		
Licked		
Like		
Lollipop		
Laughed		
Looking		
Legs		
Licking		

Not underlined

Word (reason underlined)	Reason/explanation
Flavour	Two consonant sounds together without a vowel in between (or a blend)
Blue	
Clear	
Glass	
Slowly	
Swir**ls**	
Wel**c**ome	
Quic**kl**y	

Jasper the Badger - Targeting the /j/ Sound

- While reading the story to the child, you could occasionally point out the /j/ sound e.g. "Jasper the badger loved to just sit" ... "oh, Jasper starts with a /j/ sound."

- You could talk about how <u>you</u> make the sound e.g. "I touch the tip of my tongue behind my teeth, then let it go and blow out, with my voice turned on ... /j/."

- You could get the child to watch you make the /j/ sound, and use a mirror so they can see if they are doing the same as you.

- If the child repeats the word or sound after you correctly, be sure to praise them e.g. "Well done, that was a great /j/ sound." Be sure to focus on the positive rather than the negative – don't point out their mistakes.

- You will notice some 'j' letters underlined as well as 'dg' and 'g'. In these particular words, these letters indicate a /j/ sound.

Underlined /j/ sound within words

Initial (beginning)	Medial (middle)	Final (end)
Jasper	Badger	Porridge
Just	Imogen	Dodge
Jam	Pigeon	Fudge
Jelly	Fidgety	Garage
Jenny	Imagined	Sledge
Giraffe	Nudging	Nudge
Jumpy		Huge
Juicy		Rage
Jumped		Hedge
Joy		
Jackpot		
Juggling		
Jiggled		
Jumper		
Jenny's		
Giant		
Jump		

Not underlined

Word (reason underlined)	Reason/explanation
En**j**oyed Ora**ng**e En**j**oying Mana**ged**	Two consonant sounds together without a vowel in between (blend)

Platypus and Fly - Targeting /l/ Blends

- While reading the story to the child, you could occasionally point out the /l/ sound in words with blends e.g. "Platypus is asleep" … "oh, platypus has a /l/ sound in it, do you hear it? Platypus – it starts with a /p/ and then a /l/."

- You could talk about how <u>you</u> make the sound e.g. "I touch the tip of my tongue to the roof of my mouth and roll it. I also turn my voice on … /l/."

- You could get the child to watch you make the /l/ sound, and use a mirror so they can see if they are doing the same as you. You could then make the beginning sound of the word, and practise putting the two together. (In /l/ blends, the /l/ sound is generally the second sound of the blend.)

- If the child repeats the word or sound after you correctly, be sure to praise them e.g. "Well done, that was a great /l/ sound." Be sure to focus on the positive rather than the negative – don't point out their mistakes.

- Often children may drop a sound with words that start with an /l/ blend. This may be the /l/, or it may be the sound the word starts with e.g. the /p/ in 'plate'. Sometimes it may be a different sound used all together. This story is to bring attention to both the sounds in the blend, and give the opportunity to practise using /l/ blends in words.

Underlined /l/ blends within words – all in initial position (except for one – 'asleep')

Bl	Pl	Sl	Gl	Fl	Cl
Blue	Platypus	Sleek	Gleams	Flapping	Clap
Black	Playing	Sleeps		Flying	Clean
Bleak	Place	Slowly		Fly	Clear
	Planked	Slit		Flitting	Cleaned
	Plate	Slap		Flapped	Closed
	Plank	Asleep		Flew	
	Plain			Flower	
	Play			Flee	
				Flap	
				Flit	
				Flown	
				Flitted	

The Dragon Drawing War - Targeting /r/ Blends

- While reading the story to the child, you could occasionally point out the /r/ sound in words with blends e.g. "The dragon drawing war" … "oh, dragon has a /r/ sound in it, do you hear it? Dragon. It starts with a /d/ sound and then a /r/ sound – /dr/."

- You could talk about how <u>you</u> make the sound e.g. "I touch the middle of my tongue to the sides of my teeth and curl the tip a bit … /r/."

- You could get the child to watch you make the /r/ sound, and use a mirror so they can see if they are doing the same as you. You could then make the beginning sound of the word, and practise putting the two together. (In /r/ blends, the /r/ sound is generally the second sound of the blend.)

- If the child repeats the word or sound after you correctly, be sure to praise them e.g. "Well done, that was a great /r/ sound." Be sure to focus on the positive rather than the negative – don't point out their mistakes.

- Often children may drop a sound with words that start with an /r/ blend. This may be the /r/, or it may be the sound the word starts with e.g. the /p/ in 'pretty'. Sometimes it may be a different sound used all together. This story is to bring attention to both the sounds in the blend, and give the opportunity to practise using /r/ blends in words.

Underlined /r/ blends within words – all in initial position

Fr	Br	Dr	Gr	Pr	Cr	Tr
Frosty	Brother	Dragon	Grab	Practised	Create	Trickiest
Frizzy-haired	Broken	Drawing	Gripping	Prettiest	Cross	Truly
Frog	Branches	Draw	Grey	Prowling	Crouching	Trees
Frightful	Brain	Dress	Green	Proud	Creeping	Trying
Frown		Drew	Gross	Pretty	Crackling	Train
Friends		Drooping	Gripping	Prince	Crown	
From		Driving	Ground	Promise		
		Dreamed	Great			
		Dressed	Grapes			
		Drop	Growl			
		Drawings	Grand			
		Dragons	Graceful			

Not underlined

Word (reason underlined)	Reason/explanation
Through	The sound combination of /th/ and /r/ together is a bit more tricky, and not technically a blend